Wendy Worm and Grandpa's Magic

By Don Brigham, Jr.
Illustrated by Stacy Hummel

Wendy Worm and Grandpa's Magic

Copyright© 2024 Don Brigham, Jr.
ISBN: 9798320485805

All rights reserved. No part of this book may be reproduced or used in any manner without express written permission from the copyright holders except for use of quotations in a book review.

Dedicated to my fave Daughter Felicity- the first book created for her on what became an annual tradition.

Not so long ago
in a worm hole below
the ground lived a worm family.
This story concerns
that family of worms,
They're a cute bunch, as you can see.

THE WORM'S

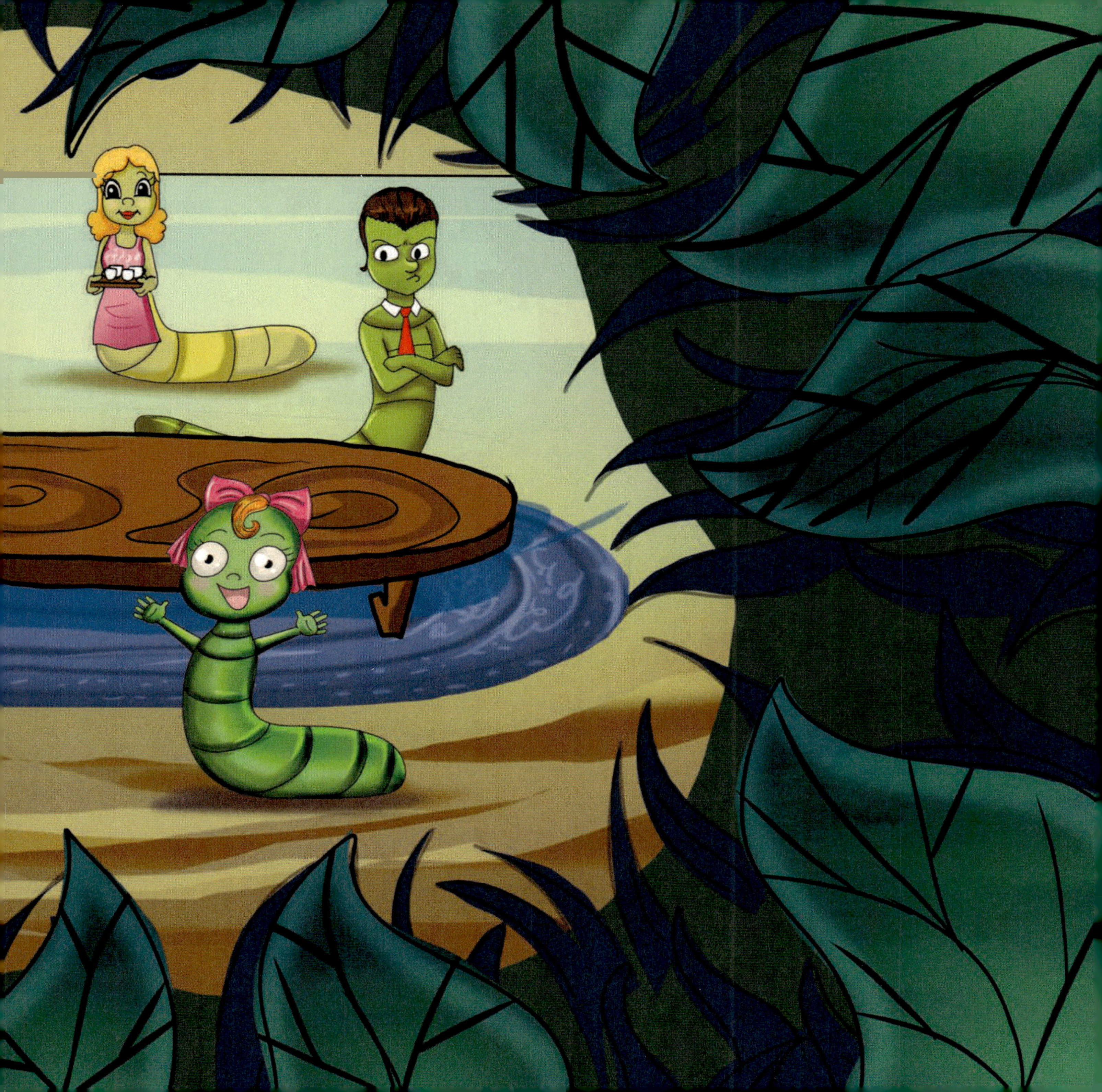

First, I'd like you to meet
little Wendy so sweet.
She's the youngest, just three years old.
She hasn't a brother,
but lives with mother
and tries to be good, good as gold.

Wendy's father lives there
He's the one with straight hair.
He works hard, but hasn't much money.
Then I have to explain
that the worm with the cane
is Grandfather (who sometimes speaks funny.)

Now the scene is all set
with the four worms you've met
in their worm cave under the ground.
As we start this strange tale
Father Worm is quite pale
he's come home and LOOK what he's found!

While he was away
Gramps decided to play
with his magic — just look what he's DONE!
Father said, with a frown,
"You've turned upside down
all our things, you ol' fool.
Was that FUN!?"

Grandad: "I'm an old worm, that's true
with not much to do
So I play my guitar and try magic.
An old worm deserves
time to rest his frayed nerves,
So, is playing with magic so tragic?"

Father: "Gramps, it's true what you say
you should have time to play
but your tricks have our house in a shamble.
Your magical spells
never work very well,
every trick you attempt is a gamble."

"Your cantations, your verse
sound more like a curse,
could it be that you've lost all your feeling?
When I want to sit down
I observe, with a frown
that my chair's overhead on the ceiling."

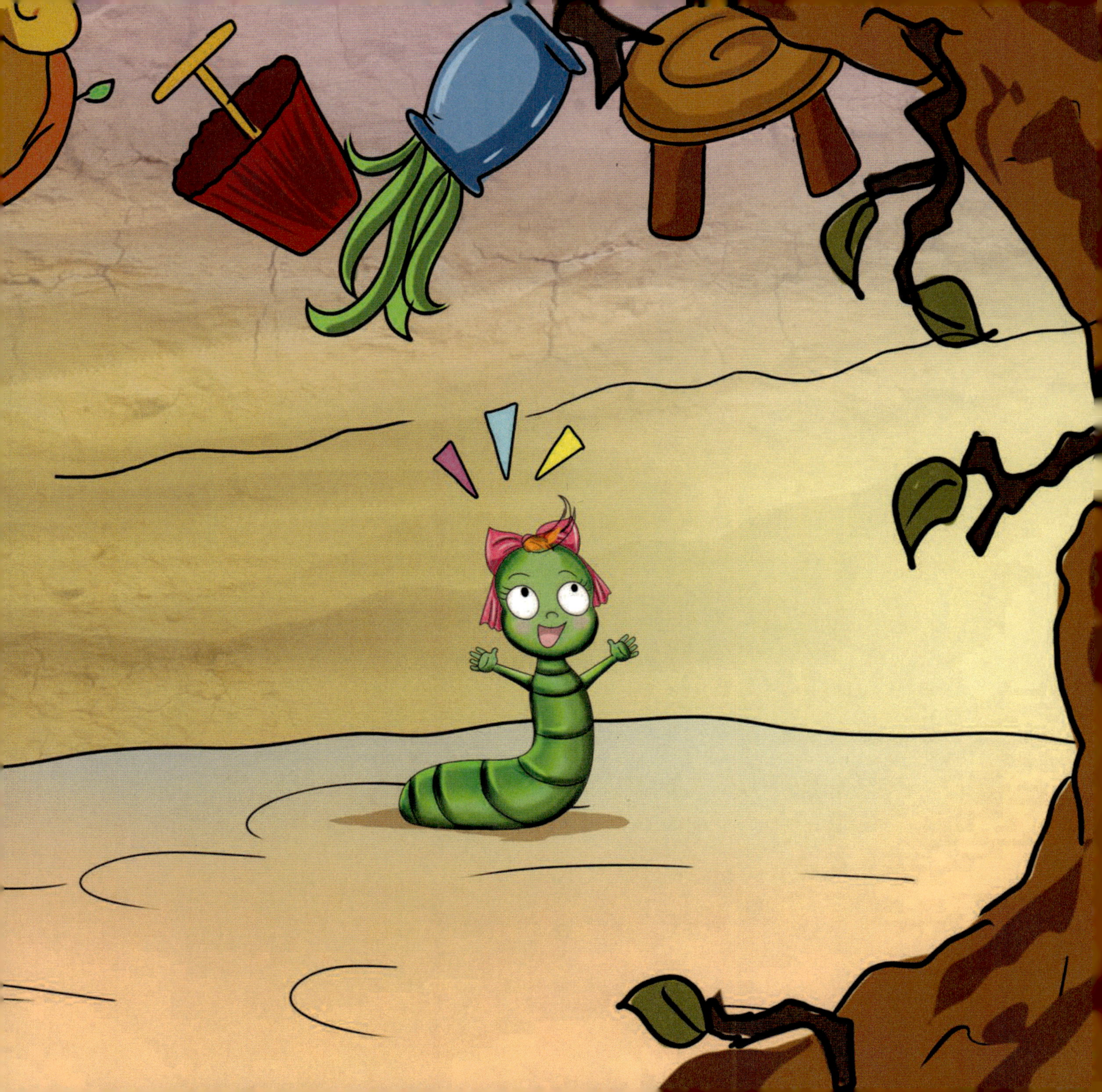

"Every **spoon**, **fork** and **plate**
and the bowl full of **dates**
are attached **upside down** way up there!
Gramps, for crying out loud!
That's a couch, not a cloud!
And where once was a **bed**, there's just **air**."

It was clear to them all
E'n the mouse down the hall
Saw that Dad was quite mad, getting madder.
He cursed and he swore
and he stomped on the floor,
All the noise made the plates start to clatter.

Father: "It seems **plain** to **me**
that you've tricked gravity;
The request that we seek is not formal:
One small favor we ask
(If you're up to the task)
Could you **PLEASE** change our house
Back to **NORMAL ?!**"

Grandpa had no reply
'cept a tear in one eye
And he said, "I'm not feeling so well.
Magic words take much thought
They take all that I've got,
So I think I'll go rest for a spell."

Then the Worm family four
they sat on the floor
looking up at their things overhead.
While alone in his room,
Gramps had a look of sad gloom
for the magic was gone from his head.

Grandpa: "Oh balloons, bees and bird's nest
Turnip greens, pears, a pink dress,
Jumpin' jacks, jeeps and jangles,
Begger's bag, bats and bangles.
Every magical word - every
Mystical phrase,
They're gone from my head
Gone kaput - I'm amazed!"

So Gramps sat on the floor
He could do nothing more.
"I will stay here and think 'til December.
I will go without sleep
That's a promise I'll keep
'til those magical words I remember."

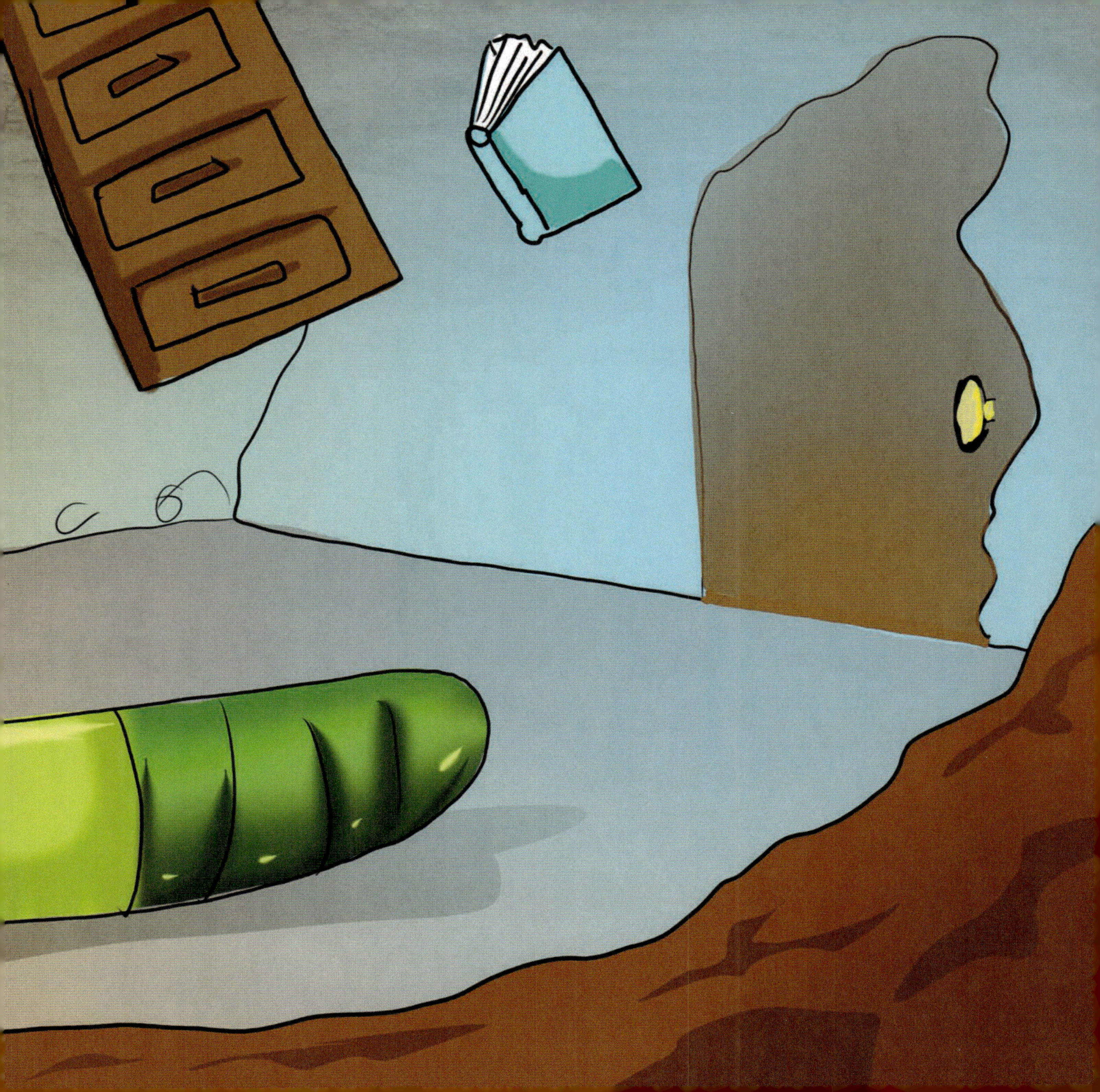

Little Wendy was sad
and her dad was still mad:
Of Gramp's magic his patience grew thin.
Wendy crawled 'cross the floor,
'cross to Grandfather's door
where she heard a sad sob from within.

"Do not cry," Wendy said
And she kissed his bald head.
"For we love you a lot – don't you know?
Let's see if we can
find the magic again,
Can I help – can we give it a go?"

Grandpa: "Thanks a lot, Wendy dear,
Now come and sit here

and together we'll work through this bad mess.
Your help I will need
if we are to succeed

or your dad will give me a new address."

Gramps held Wendy's hand
and together they planned
to recall his words from past days.
They thought for a while,
then with a shout and a smile
Gramps said, "I remember, I remember the phrase!"

"Porcupine, pits, a pansy,
Trumpet vine, tar and tansy,
Skinny shrimp, slugs-so-slimy,
Lutefisk, leaks and limey.
To you things overhead I do strongly implore
To get down from the ceiling
To get down on the floor
And return to the place that you were once before."

All the worms craned their necks
to observe the effects
of Gramp's chant — it came quick, on the double.
"Oh, no!" they exclaimed,
Then Father proclaimed,
"You old fool, now you've turned them to BUBBLES!"

Wendy said, "That's not fair,
we should show Gramps we care
and support him, but not hurt his feelings.
Before you count up to ten
Gramps will try it again.
He'll return all our stuff from the ceiling."

"One more try," Father said,
" 'cause it's clear in my head
that Gramp's magic defies explanation."
Gramps closed tight his eyes,
He drew a magical sigh
and recited a new incantation.

Lizard lips, eggs of 'gators

Lumpy oatmeal and rude waiters

Yellow snow, baby doe fur,

For dear Wendy's sake I will try one more time
My reversible magic, oh Bubbles Sublime,
You change back as you were or
I'll make more bad rhyme."

Then the bubbles all burst!
(Could things get any worse?)
So the air was just perfectly clear.

Father **yelled**, **fumed** and **pranced**

While he danced a MAD DANCE!

"All we had you have made DISAPPEAR!"

pop! *POP!* *pop!*

Gramps seemed not to mind
Father's words – so unkind.
In fact, Gramps was amused at his rage.
"You shouldn't be so quick
to yell at my trick,
there's more magic (now, please turn the page.)

"Little girls, cute and rosy

Cracklin' fires, warm and cozy.

Summer breeze, clouds so mellow

Ginkgo trees, lemon Jello.

"To complete my performance, this magic I do.
In a moment you'll see that it was good for you,
for your things will return, not as old, but BRAND NEW!"

There arose quite a cheer
as their things re-appeared.
"Our dear Grandpa is really so sweet."
Even Father had a smile,
"Gramps, you knew all the while,
I do thank you for this wonderful treat."

So, the Worm family four
was happy once more.
Father said, "Gramps, I know I was wrong.
We should be less demanding,
We should show understanding
and love each other all life long."

THE END

Made in the USA
Middletown, DE
27 July 2024

57992882R00022